WHO WOULD WIN?®

WALRUS

VS.

ELEPHANT SEAL

BY
JERRY PALLOTTA

ILLUSTRATED BY
ROB BOLSTER

Scholastic Inc.

The publisher would like to thank the following for their
kind permission to use their photographs in this book:
Photos ©: 10: mikeuk/Getty Images; 11: Kevin Schafer/Getty Images;
15: Wolfgang Kaehler/LightRocket/Getty Images; 24: Sylvain Cordier/Gamma-Rapho/Getty
Images; 25: John Eastcott and Yva Momatiuk/Getty Images.

To my favorite banker, Ellen Gillette.
—J. P.

To my favorite beachgoers, Mark and Maureen.
—R.B.

ISBN 978-1-338-67211-4

10 9 8 7 6 5 4 3 2 1   21 22 23 24 25

Printed in the U.S.A.   40
First printing, January 2021

What would happen if a walrus swam into an elephant seal? What if they had a fight? If they met on land, on ice, or in the ocean, who do you think would win?

FIN FACT
Seals are in a group of animals called pinnipeds. Pinniped means "finned feet."

MEET A WALRUS

There are two types of walruses: Atlantic walruses and Pacific walruses. Atlantic walruses range from Canada to Greenland. Scientific name: *Odobenus rosmarus rosmarus*

Atlantic walrus

The Arctic is the northernmost area of the Earth. Polar bears live in the Arctic, but not penguins. The Arctic also has walruses.

Atlantic walrus territory

NORTHERN HEMISPHERE

VIEW OF EARTH FROM ABOVE THE NORTH POLE

Africa

Europe

Asia

ARCTIC CIRCLE

North Pole

ATLANTIC OCEAN

ARCTIC OCEAN

South America

North America

PACIFIC OCEAN

MEET AN ELEPHANT SEAL

There are two kinds of elephant seals: northern elephant seals and southern elephant seals.
Scientific name: *Mirounga angustirostris*

BIG AND BIGGER
Male northern elephant seals are three times heavier than females.

northern elephant seal

Northern elephant seals live in the northern hemisphere, mostly along the western coast of the US, Mexico, and Canada.

northern elephant seal territory

NORTHERN HEMISPHERE

Africa

Europe

Asia

ARCTIC CIRCLE

North Pole

ARCTIC OCEAN

ATLANTIC OCEAN

South America

North America

PACIFIC OCEAN

VIEW OF EARTH FROM ABOVE THE NORTH POLE

MEET ANOTHER WALRUS

Pacific walruses live on the coasts of Russia and Alaska.
Scientific name: *Odobenus rosmarus*
Its scientific name means "tooth-walking seahorse."

FACT
A walrus is a seal.

Pacific walrus

VIEW OF EARTH FROM ABOVE THE NORTH POLE

NORTHERN HEMISPHERE

Pacific walrus territory

Africa

Asia

Europe

ARCTIC CIRCLE

North Pole

ARCTIC OCEAN

ATLANTIC OCEAN

South America

North America

PACIFIC OCEAN

MEET ANOTHER ELEPHANT SEAL

Southern elephant seals live in the sub-Antarctic and Antarctic. Scientific name: *Mirounga leonina*

DID YOU KNOW?
The Antarctic region has penguins, but no polar bears or walruses.

southern elephant seal

VIEW OF EARTH FROM ABOVE THE SOUTH POLE

SOUTHERN HEMISPHERE

southern elephant seal territory

Australia

ANTARCTIC CIRCLE

South Pole

Antarctica

PACIFIC OCEAN

Africa

ATLANTIC OCEAN

South America

THINK

Let's see, walruses live in the northern hemisphere, and southern elephant seals live in the southern hemisphere. They wouldn't meet in real life. But we'll let them meet in this book. The walrus in this book will be the Pacific walrus.

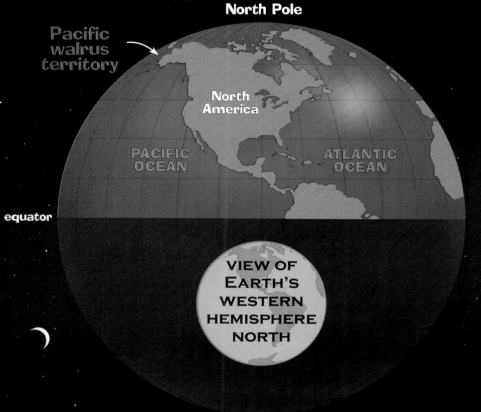

Weight and Size

Male Pacific walruses can weigh up to 4,000 lbs. They can grow up to 12 feet long.

Pacific walrus
4,000 lbs.

adult male
200 lbs.

8

DECIDE

From now on the elephant seal in this book will be the southern elephant seal.

VIEW OF
EARTH'S
WESTERN
HEMISPHERE
SOUTH

equator

South America

PACIFIC OCEAN

ATLANTIC OCEAN

southern elephant seal territory

Antarctica

South Pole

Weight and Size

Male southern elephant seals can weigh up to 8,800 lbs. They can grow more than 20 feet long. The southern elephant seal is the largest carnivorous mammal that is not a whale.

DEFINITION
A carnivore is an animal that eats meat.

first-grade girl
52 lbs.

southern elephant seal
8,800 lbs.

TUSKS

What is most noticeable about walruses? Their tusks! Walrus tusks can be more than 3 feet long. Tusks help walruses defend themselves from killer whales or polar bears.

Another noticeable thing about walruses? Their long whiskers.

WHISKER FACT
Walruses' whiskers are called vibrissae. The whiskers pick up vibrations in the water and on the ocean floor.

Walruses, like other earless seals, have earholes in the side of their heads but no earflaps.

ear hole

EAR FACT
There are two types of seals: earless seals and eared seals.

ear flap

SNOUT

What is most noticeable about male elephant seals?
Their snouts. They are used mostly for making noise.

SNOUT FACT
*Female elephant
seals do not have an
enlarged snout.*

Elephant seals are also earless seals. They have
no earflaps.

MORE TUSKS

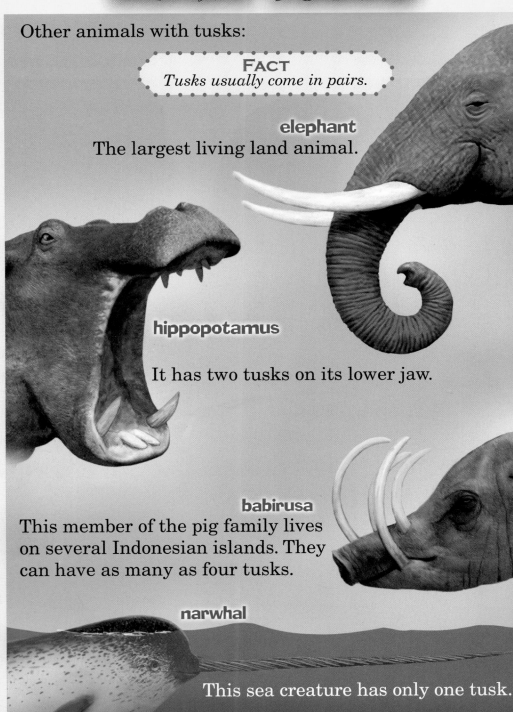

Other animals with tusks:

elephant

The largest living land animal.

hippopotamus

It has two tusks on its lower jaw.

babirusa

This member of the pig family lives on several Indonesian islands. They can have as many as four tusks.

narwhal

This sea creature has only one tusk.

OTHER SNOUTS

Other animals with enlarged snouts:

BONUS FACT
An elephant has 40,000 muscles in its trunk.

elephant

tapir

proboscis monkey

elephant shrew

FAT

Walrus skin is up to 1.5 inches thick. Walrus blubber, or fat, is up to 4 inches thick. Blubber keeps walruses warm. Walruses can comfortably swim in freezing-cold water or sit on ice without getting cold.

DEFINITION
Blubber is the fat in sea mammals.

actual size

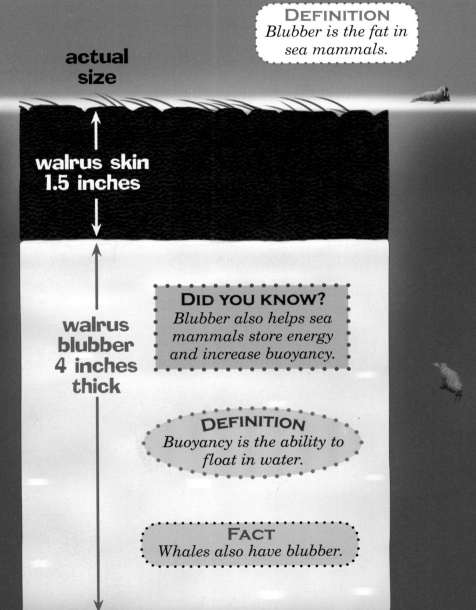

walrus skin
1.5 inches

walrus blubber
4 inches thick

DID YOU KNOW?
Blubber also helps sea mammals store energy and increase buoyancy.

DEFINITION
Buoyancy is the ability to float in water.

FACT
Whales also have blubber.

BLUBBER

Elephant seals also have thick skin and a layer of blubber. While many mammals grow new hair and skin over time, an elephant seal replaces their skin and fur all at once. Every year elephant seals molt, or replace, their fur.

CONSERVATION FACT
Sea mammals are protected by the Marine Mammal Protection Act.

DID YOU KNOW?
Elephant seal blubber was often used to make lamp oil.

WALRUS PARTS

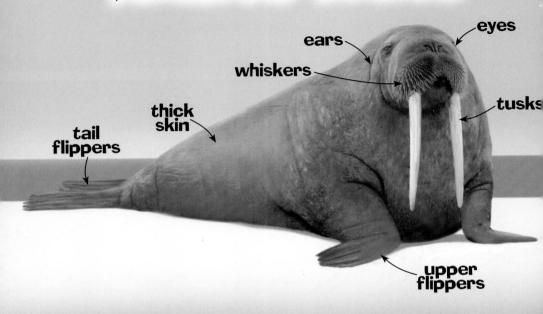

eyes

ears

whiskers

tusks

thick skin

tail flippers

upper flippers

BABY FACT
A baby walrus is called a pup or calf.

baby walrus

WELCOME TO THE WORLD, BABY WALRUS!

BORN: SPRINGTIME
HOME: NEAR THE ARCTIC
WEIGHT: 100–165 LBS.
LENGTH: 3.5–5 FT.
DISTINGUISHING FEATURE: MUSTACHE
INSTEAD OF CLAMS. PLEASE SEND HUGS.

ELEPHANT SEAL PARTS

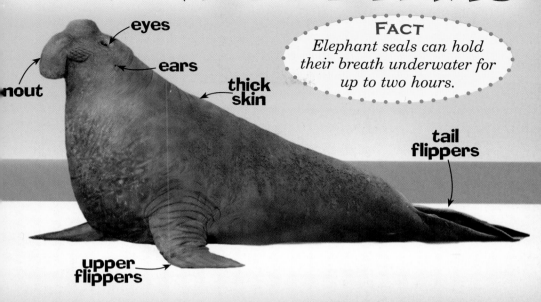

eyes

ears

snout

thick skin

tail flippers

upper flippers

FACT
Elephant seals can hold their breath underwater for up to two hours.

BABY FACT
A baby elephant seal is called a pup.

baby elephant seal

WELCOME NEW BABY!

OUR CUTE BABY ELEPHANT SEAL WEIGHED 80 LBS. AT BIRTH!

FLIPPERS

Walruses do not have arms and legs; they have flippers. They propel themselves in the water with their tail flippers. They steer with their upper flippers.

> ### FLIPPER FACT
> *Fur seals steer with their tails and swim with their upper flippers.*

> ### FACT
> *Walruses can hold their breath underwater for up to 10 minutes.*

SPEED

On land, walruses crawl slowly, only about 5 mph. They're much faster in the water, swimming up to 22 mph.

swimming

SPEED LIMIT 5

crawling

SPEED LIMIT 22

WEBBING

Flippers of elephant seals have five digits. Their "fingers" are webbed.

upper flipper

tail flipper

FLIPPER FACT

Like walruses, elephant seals also propel themselves with their tail flippers and steer with upper flippers.

SPEED

Elephant seals are also slow on land, flopping at about 5 mph. But they swim quickly, reaching speeds of 10–15 mph. The fastest human swimmers reach only about 5–6 mph.

crawling

SPEED LIMIT 5

swimming

SPEED LIMIT 15

AWESOME SEAL FACTS

Smallest Seal

The nerpa is the smallest seal in the world.

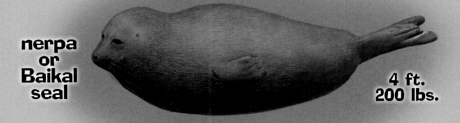

nerpa or Baikal seal

4 ft. 200 lbs.

Smallest Ocean Seal

The smallest ocean seal is the ringed seal.

ringed seal

5 ft. 200 lbs.

MORE ABOUT SEALS

tanker

DIVE FACT
Elephant seals can dive down to 1 mile deep searching for food.

iceberg

HISTORY FACT
Elephant seals were almost hunted to extinction for the oil in their blubber.

oil lamp

DEFINITION
Extinction is when a species dies out completely.

1 mile

COMPARE

Here is a walrus skull. Walruses eat mostly clams.

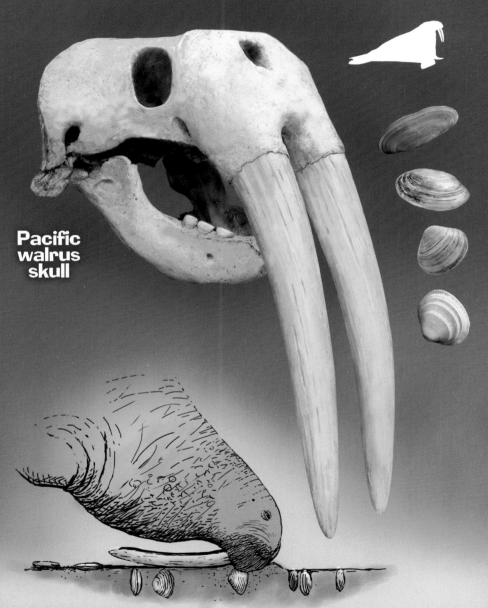

Pacific
walrus
skull

They find clams buried in the sand using their whiskers.
A walrus's mouth is designed like a vacuum cleaner to
suck the clams out of their shells.

CONTRAST

Here is a southern elephant seal skull. Elephant seals eat fish, squid, sharks, and other seals.

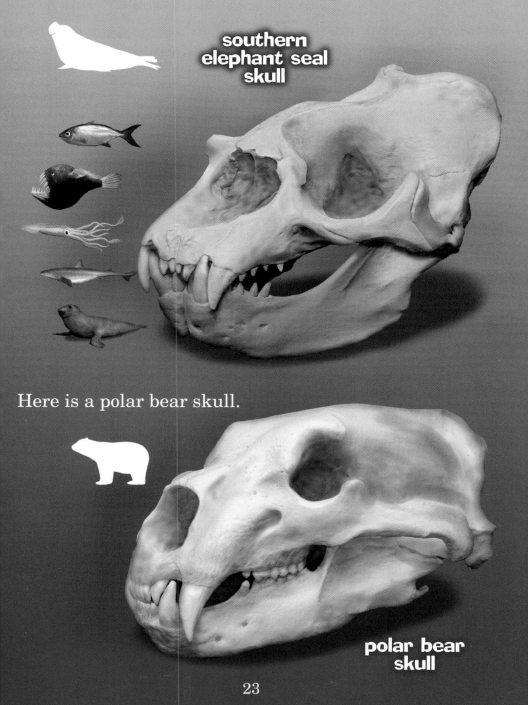

southern elephant seal skull

Here is a polar bear skull.

polar bear skull

HUDDLE

When walruses want to protect their pups from polar bears, the adults get in a circle and surround their young ones. It is called a huddle of walruses.

GEOGRAPHIC FACT
A walrus has never seen a penguin. A penguin has never seen a polar bear.

SLEEP FACT
Walruses have been known to sleep for up to 19 hours straight.

COLONY

On land, a large group of elephant seals is called a colony. Here is a colony of elephant seals.

LAND FACT

On land, a group of seals could also be called a harem or a rookery.

A large group of seals in the water is called a raft of seals.

DUEL ON LAND

The walrus and the elephant seal are on a beach. They flop, or bounce, while moving. On land they both move more slowly than in water.

The walrus threatens the elephant seal with its long tusks.

The elephant seal is much larger and heavier. It shoves the walrus. The elephant seal is not afraid—it smashes its huge body into the walrus.

It has no trouble pushing the walrus around.

On land, the elephant seal wins.

CLASH ON ICE

Here is a big ice floe. The walrus uses its tusks to pull itself up on the ice. The elephant seal sees the walrus.

DEFINITION
A floe is a sheet of floating ice.

The elephant seal swims around the ice deciding what to do. It tries to climb on the ice floe.

The elephant seal is too heavy to pull itself up on the ice. The walrus uses its tusks to bang the seal's head.

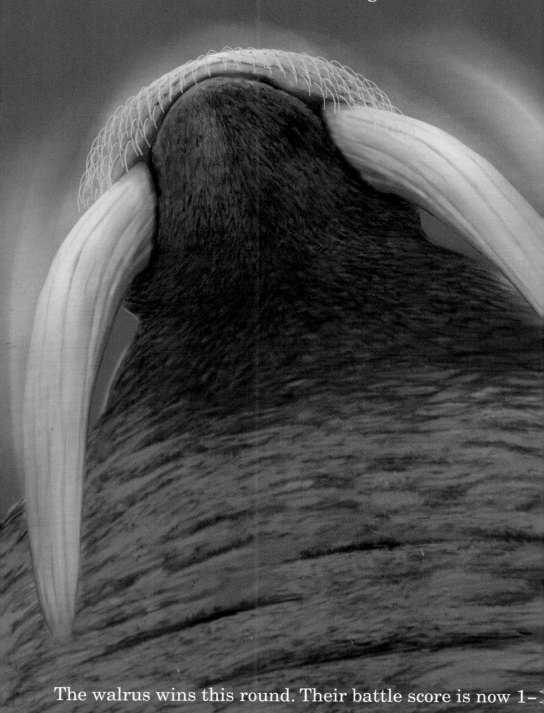

The walrus wins this round. Their battle score is now 1–1

BATTLE IN WATER

In the water the elephant seal has an advantage—it can hold its breath longer than a walrus can. The elephant seal is so heavy it can push the walrus around.

The elephant seal bites the walrus. The walrus has thick skin, but it is wounded. The elephant seal uses its size advantage to push the walrus underwater.

The elephant seal rams the walrus. Boom! Boom! The elephant seal hurts the walrus. The fight is over. The elephant seal has won two of the three battles. Elephant seal wins!

WHO HAS THE ADVANTAGE? CHECKLIST

WALRUS		ELEPHANT SEAL
☐	Size	☐
☐	Tusks	☐
☐	Weight	☐
☐	Land Speed	☐
☐	Ocean Speed	☐
☐	Diving	☐
☐	Breath Holding	☐

If you were the author, how would you write the ending?